03 YELLOW • **BOOK 9** /ar/

Minneapolis, Minnesota

Teaching Tips

This book focuses on the phoneme **/ar/**.

Getting Started

- Review the focus phoneme of the book with readers.
- Model the sound and have readers practice themselves.

Using the Book

- Ask readers to read the words on the pages with the colorful borders, using the focus sound as their guide.
- Turn the page and check the illustration next to the word to confirm accuracy.
- As you read new words, review the word bank on the left-hand pages of the book.

Reviewing

- Encourage readers to independently reread all of the words on pages 22–23.
- Have them complete the activity on page 24 for continued practice with the focus phoneme.
- Extend the learning by asking readers if they know any other words containing the focus phoneme.

© 2025 Booklife Publishing
This edition is published by arrangement with Booklife Publishing.

North American adaptations © 2025 Bearport Publishing Company. All rights reserved. No part of this publication may be reproduced in whole or in part, stored in any retrieval system, or transmitted in any form or by any means, electronic, mechanical, photocopying, recording, or otherwise, without written permission from the publisher. Bearport Publishing is a division of Chrysalis Education Group.

For more information, write to Bearport Publishing, 5357 Penn Avenue South, Minneapolis, MN 55419.

bark

bark

bark

barn

barn

barn

bark

barn

bar

bar

bar

bark

barn

bar

car

car

car

bark
barn
bar
car
dart

dart

dart

bark

 barn

bar

 car

 dart

Read the words on the left. Trace your finger from each word to its matching picture.

dart

bar

car